THE RING ROAD

A POETIC SEQUENCE

*To Frankie
with all good wishes,
Jonathan*

JONATHAN ALDRICH

27 Oct 08

LIMEROCK BOOKS

Limerock Books • 15 Mechanic Street • Thomaston, ME 04861
limebks@gmail.com

The Ring Road: A Poetic Sequence

ISBN: 978-0-9746589-3-3

Cover photo: "In St. Stephen's Green, Dublin," Jonathan Aldrich

The poems on pages 18, 24 and 99 previously appeared
in *Summer Lines: A Decade of Tenants Harbor Poetry Readings*,
Limerock Books, 2006

Printed in the USA by Custom Museum Publishing,
479 Main Street, Rockland, ME 04841

First Edition

Only a single, soft
cloud appeared in the sky
the day that you were born.
They say all afternoon
it hung aloft,

an anomaly in the blue
and almost windless weather,
finally settling vaguely
westward and overhead.
It liked the view

(that long ago July)
of farms and drumlin hills
and county roads, the white,
black-shuttered family homestead.
A single cloud in the sky.

CONTENTS

ONE

In summer the fireflies
come from the meadow up,
blinking from where they all
began?—and yet my brother
and I think otherwise:

They have huddled in our trees
and gradually grown
restive and cool and eager
to give back the moonlight,
becoming fireflies

to float in total ease,
although we can't explain
the occasional shortfall
before they come again,
touching our busy days.

So many gods pour out
of the sky on autumn nights,
pounding and flashing, the placid
prints my mother has hung
in the hall seem incomplete.

A child ogles the sunrise
in one print. In another
he holds a conch to his ear.
Next he tests a strawberry.
Now he presses his nose

to some flower on a trellis.
Then strokes a fluffy rabbit...
So go the sensible gods.
But there are more than five
gods, these evenings tell us.

The goblins underneath
our house want it their way,
tunneled and wayward, many
with hatchets and mallets they
chuckle under their breath.

Some casual remark
brought forth the hard-working goblins.
No moonbeams ever reach
the cellar, where on a full moon
I hear them chipping rock.

The world I would replace
tonight won't go away.
It's here to stay. It is
deeper than you, than I am,
deeper than any of us.

Would I grow up to write
philosophy to dispel
once and for all
dilemmas of the day,
old riddles of the night?

Here at my winter window
I thought of the fountain pen
I'd dropped and scrounged in leaves for,
later in snow. "Oh well,
it's rusty and gone by now."

Being eleven or so,
at least I thought I knew
every word in the English language
because I could never think
of any I didn't know.

White snow against the red
berries, or the other way
around: I was a little
tyke at the time, grade school
at the end of the road.

Miss Miller hated the snow,
she spoke of that fact, and how
she hated "things in bloom,"
checking us into home room.
She had nowhere to go.

One day she drank the red
wine from her cupboard, I'm told.
I do not think it was wine,
it was too hot, too cold
at the end of the road.

A man with my first name
was traveling overland
at night by horse-drawn coach
when bats began to flap
in mist ahead of him.

Quite luckily he kept
a Journal, and so we know
the story in his own words.
For many nights I read
his words before I slept

and remember to this day
a man with my first name
alone on a driverless coach
and how the bats began
to beat, leading the way.

These are my grandmother's
false teeth apparently.
On a low shelf between
our pantry and cellarway
they soak in one of the jars.

They do not smile. Of course
she doesn't smile much either.
And now that she's asleep
upstairs I can assume
she's smiling even less.

Yes, one two three four five
etc., I count
dead teeth in her small jaw
before she's back downstairs
to be talking and alive.

Music is still a mystery
like the stars and planets.
Many who write of music
tell us largely about
its being far away

or suddenly overheard,
as if it were not here—
as if we could ignore
either its harmony or
destruction. But when he untied

his little boat, leaving
willow and bank, and rowed
out onto the dark lake
below high cliffs he felt life's
mathematical breathing.

If holiday turkey is sliced
extremely thin it doesn't
necessarily taste
any better. If antique
ladderback chairs are placed

close to facilitate
adult conversation and the
circulation of Mary
it doesn't necessarily
help you to sit up straight.

Everything we're able
to say about family starts
with food: the kind of food,
the amount, the server,
the way we're joined at table.

Her toe on the carpet. A buzz,
and almost instantly
Hannon appears, to clear
dessert, and everything is
exactly as it was

except for dirty napkins
and a spot on the tablecloth
where my blueberry pie had been.
Never can I escape it!
I hate the way my sins

are uncovered, one by one,
and registered by those
who glance away—my sins
uncovered one by one
and not remarked upon.

Leaving his family, a child
walks through an alley courtyard
where ashcans tilt. Grass tufts
skewer the mildewed brick.
Although he smells a mild

piss, it's refreshing because
the standards are not high here.
Someone has left the gate open.
Nobody cares or knows much
what anyone says or does.

So it's pleasant to be
passing servanted homes
unseen—only myself
spotting the weeds and dog-poop
and swill of a week's debris.

They said a stranger hid
and leapt from trees. "Springtime!"
one of the jock-boys joked,
who hadn't seen him.
None of us had.

April already, bush
and crocus in bloom, night rains
washing the riverbank
and lifting the wide river.
Some of the girls were hushed

or giggling. "He shows his tool!"
And did the night rains wash
him, too? What beauty or blood
or danger swelled the Charles
I walked along to school?

The world is off, and we
don't know the tilt of Heaven;
can hardly explain even
why the whitethroat sings
on certain days only.

Each odd discrepancy
issues from afar, and
among the family toys
and gatherings I see
kind Greatie at 93

leaning secretly near
one sunny Easter morning
and whispering, "The rain
is making so much noise.
Doesn't it bother you, dear?"

I fear we are greatly fooled,
the Buddha said, by the twitter
of sparrows, lakewater
lapping on shores, the sun
itself: only a child

believes a thunder clap
or rain with a summer romp
or a flower on the hill
or the touch of brightening sky
at dawn can anticipate

a world of easiness
for anyone, because
no one believes these things
are real—except a child,
or lingering childishness.

I say a dream is like
an ancient olive tree
that never dies, sending
continous roots out
underground before I wake,

before the dreamer wakes,
roots popping up forever
to make new olive trees
on other grounds. Asleep
I let a wild red fox

slip from his hedge at dawn,
pause, sniff the gorse and break
into an easy trot
across an open field heedless
of any hunter's plan.

Although his talk was always
superficial, my grandfather
had kindness and good humor.
I liked his lackadaisical
half-penurious ways,

I liked his motorboat
called Puffin, often moored
all morning, all day long
and riding pointlessly
the harbor waves—and yet

once early every summer
my grandfather and brother
and I, beyond Mosquito
and Green and Little Green,
pulled cod from the deep water.

TWO

Remember the rogue wave
that swept Jenny away?
As a child thoroughly dipped
in movieland I saw
it coming—no way to save

Jenny, to save her life!
Today that movie-house
is gone, taking its faithful
dusty cone of light.
I cannot learn to scoff

at the old days, I cannot learn
to give up Jennifer Jones.
If innocence is gone
(or drowned) somewhere the reels
go spinning on and on.

The young fall in love instantly,
as surely as the stars
rise and a whippoorwill
calls nightly, just before nine.
And as for himself, he

sees her walking the market
square and talking to someone
who doesn't look familiar
before she approaches the theater,
or is she buying a ticket?

An old and bitter-sweet story,
to fall in love instantly.
Later it was the way
she sat at table, her hands.
He was no longer free.

Letting her underthings
drop to the floor, she puts on
a bathing suit—it's tight
in the crotch. Okay, let 'em watch
and see how the cloth clings.

Now she pretends to be
oblivious, swinging her legs
over the beach and circling
volleyballers, who are proud
of their tight buns probably.

She is outside and inside
herself simultaneously.
She is playing volleyball.
She is eating a hot dog.
She is swimming with the tide.

First only a few feathers
of darkness,
which you can brush from your eyes.
Then in that fluttering it
gets darker still, as sleek as

onyx, soft as velvet.
Starting in darkness it
gets darker until it grows
enveloping—until
a deep envelope of night

is sealed. Is there a letter
deeper that you haven't read yet?
Maybe. Starting in darkness
it gets darker. Staying
in darkness it gets darker.

If days are chasing one
illusion after another
(butterflies—words—the soul—
ah yes, such butterflies!)
is everything an illusion?

Better than anything else
at first, our early days
arrived like particles
in space before they came
together in meaning and faults.

No more do they feel new.
Perhaps they really do
snap shut like a little box,
the way the poet Yeats
wanted his verses to.

I feel them both—a warm
breeze and the leftover
coolness of 5 AM
as I begin to jog
down from the sleepy farm.

Temperature comes in layers,
one wafted on another.
Oh it'll be a scorcher,
I can assume already
from the two airs.

Empty and quiet, only
the faintest forest birdsong,
this is the one untrammeled
hour the whole day long.
You wouldn't call it lonely.

I wish I could find an answer
in the articulate grass
to satisfy me finally.
I call the grass articulate
because at dusk I hear

crickets that almost sound
like your heels—the sliding click
of heels as you left and entered
the subway—and I've seen
a mole running underground,

an occasional sparrow pecking
for seed, and also in certain
areas ants. But I don't,
don't see an answer beyond
these ordinary things.

What is withheld, what known,
teacup and timberline,
fiery dawn. The man
who smoked his cigarette
last night may *not* be gone,

a pulsing red dot of light
across the lake, a man
sitting on his front porch
and watching you watch him,
hardly moving all night.

Now he's thought better of it.
Where has he gone? A stillness
that some would call beautiful
invades the water. No wave
to ruffle, no wind to move it.

Better to wear your sword
as long as you can, George Fox
advises. Another man calls
it better to be a violent
fool than to be a coward.

It's all a process, done
imperfectly at best,
like managing your ego:
you need an ego first
and preferably a good one.

Nothing you want is false
or stupid, even a sun
shining without clouds. In nature
the bud grows, the flower
breaks, the leaf falls.

Nor are the 59
slogans of Atisha
to be ignored. Some run:
Rest in the nature of alaya,
the essence. In post-meditation

be a child of illusion.
Don't talk about injured limbs.
Abandon hope of fruition.
Meditate on whatever
provokes resentment. Train

without bias in all areas.
Don't misinterpret. Don't
vacillate. Train whole-heartedly.
Don't wallow in self-pity.
Don't expect applause.

The piano she has moved
to the far corner of the living room
is the family's walnut upright
that casts away the gloom
of memories she loved.

It's full of the quaint songs
that somehow she doesn't hear
right now—old songs that wait
in readiness, like "Peg o' My Heart,"
torn sheet music that belongs

to herself now. The piano
is versatile, telling her of
grandparents and her childhood,
a farmhouse. Some nights it contains
all she wants to know.

Needing another kind
of beauty, what is the eye?
More than mere cornea,
iris, eyelid, cilia,
pupil, duct to the tear gland,

it wears an unconfessed
intelligence of its own,
and mine, like anyone's,
is sometimes on the prowl
for more than just

daylight—like the eye
peeping from cellar wine bins
in "The Spiral Staircase" wanting
the cripple, the waif, error,
any half-wit graffiti.

Not by the orchard's smell
or the warm nights could we
predict this wild profusion
already moving on.
Soon fields will be "beautiful

in snow," if you like the earth
covered with nothingness
and a cold wind blowing
west or east or any
whichway for all it's worth.

Some see a single bud
form and gather and blossom
and die in the logic of days.
And some will let a question
go and believe in God.

In our window the Christ child,
a few straightforward chunks
of leaded glass to form
a glowing 6" oval—
an early token sold

in Paris to my grandmother:
of yellows, purples, reds
and blues, a painted face
and swaddling bands (although
she bought it only for

—she said—the kind expression);
and if we ever had
a house-fire I would run
to save it, I wouldn't have
it lost or melted down.

Some have taken the lapse
seriously, of Good and Evil,
that disappearing act,
but him, he hardly minds it,
pondering in his cups

the earlier way it was.
Now laundry flaps on a bough;
days wrinkle and blow—
nothing of any particular
use or value. Does

this bother him much? Not very.
He draws bathwater and
steps in. He washes. Brushes
his teeth. The moon
rises like a berry.

Say you're meandering
all day upcountry when
you fall into a maze
of hedges you get lost in
trailing a gold string.

You find a creature sleeping.
Day is almost done,
and as an eye slides open
you see only a black sun
and hear a distant clipping

and frantically at nightfall
follow the gold string out.
Try as you will to wake
you join us in the dark,
oh brother animal.

When a kaleidoscope
that was the world's toy breaks
and spills out glass there is
no good looking for pictures
or scooping the glass up,

no good, the pieces don't
even reflect light now
but lie cloudy and dull, as if
swirls of scattering seawater
had left them irrelevant

to anything else here,
lost and cloudy and dull,
and we can remember only
familiar patterns, like
a land immersed in war.

It folds into the mind
like a piece of paper folding
vaguely this way and that,
like laundry in the wind,
and loosely undefined

as it was always so.
Even your childhood days
will honor it always;
at times your later age
allows it. Even now

if you should reach your hand
to what you think you want
it will be there, like a piece
of paper folding and still
like laundry in the wind.

The underground is good.
Purgatory and Hell
are here above, flourishing
their dark flowers of evil.
All shall be understood

as we drop underground.
Today I see a girl
dialing a telephone.
She knows from the I.D.
somebody else has phoned

but doesn't recognize
the number. What cannot
be said cannot be said,
and she is alive, not dead.
Heaven is in her eyes.

THREE

I can hardly see you
with the light off, but I see
our tank illuminated,
hear its buzzing. I see
a blue and orange fish who

flickers a plume of gills,
easing its lacy way
through weeds and compatriots
down to the fallen feed
and yellow pebbles,

down to those pebbles we
sifted the other day,
down through the greenery
and tufts and wafting bubbles
to make a discovery.

These are the warm shadows
we like to anticipate
riding over sea
and hill and city
as the brief summer goes.

Our trees begin to blow
at night with less to say.
The ruffled branches make
on every lawn
their usual little dumb-show

no less shadowy than
our bedroom windowshade
caging the moonlight, no
less shadowy than the words
I write, pages I turn.

Eludes me. Let it go.
You ask me to explain
(over and over again?)
our underwater life.
But this I cannot do,

unless some evening we,
swimming together, emerge
and walk awhile and reach
an opening, surely to find
some new contradictory

smokiness over the land,
a swirl and tapping of birds.
I only say that words
won't take us there. This much
I think you understand.

Rubbing my eyes and nearly
half awake I stumble
down to the living room
and rub my eyes again.
You must have got up early

to bring back violets
and small wildflowers wet
with dew (these early sunrises
in summers seem to be more
enticing than the sunsets).

Your kindness is a given,
but where are you now? I take
my usual coffee, sit
where you have kept our living
room a room to live in.

"Oh, no, the intellectual
cannot be happy," so gurus
are claiming time and again
and always I think they mean
me, singling me out. Well,

I have thought long on this,
having taken many a lump
from gurus. Sure, I analyze
and think, and sometimes even
over a nightcap pause

to ponder the Final Cause.
I go to bed serene.
I wake up ready to jump
for joy. Perhaps I'm not
as smart as I thought I was.

What focus the man had,
tapping his simple songs
away in elegant spats
and coattails, ever the savvy
ace or impeccable cad

catching the girl or not.
Ah, yes! Of course we know
practice alone makes easy
(or easy-seeming) and also
there's many a fine pursuit

better than scaling stairways
flipping a cane or doffing
your hat to a lady and
happily singing your heart out.
How have we spent our days?

Like a mobile over
a crib in Kentucky once
my early tales are lost
to you, of Policeman
Parker, the undercover

savior of little Peebo
who always wandered off
too far and became lost.
Ritual stories. Quietly
told, they gave a placebo

effect to the bedtime air
balancing like the muted
red and blue and magenta
ovals and hearts that moved
you to sleep like prayer.

My daughter felt that poison
ivy would float off the leaves
and *kill* by fuming the air
with gas—when she was five
or six—and for this reason

despite my disclaimers, each
of us agreed to give
that area a wide berth,
letting the groundcover sprawl.
Another "sinister patch"

lay near our property
shiny tight-curled in spring
and redder and rich in fall.
Passing in mid July
we took hands and moved quickly.

Mrs. Christie hopes we'll
forget she dipped into the mind
of the murderer early on,
not very long or much, but
enough to have cheated a little,

fueling a sympathy for
Evil—a sympathy not
quite right, my son will agree,
listening carefully now,
his eyes on a ceiling-crack or

a shaded window. We're
not talking *Roger Ackroyd*
or the detective-murderer here,
which the bedtime boy and I
consider entirely fair.

In praise of folly?—yes,
we knew it once. Better
than spinning a reason out
or needing to be right.
Better than loneliness.

Folly is folly. It brings
a father's photographs,
and wrapped in ribbons are
a mother's diaries
when you said funny things.

One summer standing after
a shower as breezes rippled
tall grass and all
the flowers bent your way
you heard an endless laughter.

The double-chalice of
the sand timer that came
with our new Scrabble set
is fine but irrelevant.
It's simpler to forgive

the waiting turn to turn,
although as I shuffle a few
letters around for want
of anything better to do
in the interim, I imagine

pebble and rock and boulder
and sand of those ancient
generations of aborigines
who also awaited the word,
feeling the years turn over.

God of unknown, of days
unlimited—although
how limited they seem!—
I must apologize
for my unsettled ways.

And yet God made me so,
the way I am. And of
the many things I've done
badly, daughter, I must
apologize to you

for any sufferings
created by my words
one angry evening. Trust
is so easily wiped away
like dust on dragonfly wings.

And he saw they were not happy.
It saddened him to see
his children sad—sad not
about death or illness but
rather about something he

could hardly diagnose.
It came, perhaps, from little
gaps and spaces, staring
out at a rough ocean
or into the black trees

too long or not long enough—
not from the usual
comprehendible blows
or losses in the so-called
tragedies of life.

Now the mirror only
belittles the face, and explains
nothing of time or place
or reason for pains.
The favorite statue by

Degas, La Petite Danseuse
—a photo above the jars—
quietly gives the lie
to real ballet slippers here.
Never is there applause;

a compliment brings tears.
Young girl tying her hair.
Oh where is the dance,
where is the dancer's grace,
thought to come with years?

Still there is only one
garden for each of us
whose light falls perfectly.
Although this garden slips
away it is not forgotten,

and while we carry many
bundles of flowers from one
new garden to another,
I want to tell you, children,
you won't discover any

to outdo the first
that lay unpicked and waiting.
Remember: there is only
one garden where the moon
came up and the sun burst.

FOUR

Our neighborhood is changing
for the better in some ways—
fine people, fewer trees
to shed in November. Still
I'd rather be arranging

another trip. I like
ruins and sacred places.
Once there was Avebury
where our kids tumbled around
all afternoon before dark,

barrow, menhir, down,
the stones hewn roughly up
on hills, you couldn't see
them all at once, a motion
furtively serpentine.

Why didn't I go in
and join the locals nursing
Guinness and Harp, a dozen
old geezers and two others
at fiddle and accordion

hunched at the smoky end
of a bench—old regulars
spotting me in the doorway
of the small pub O'Keefe's
in Cooraclare, who turned

with the eyes of one man
curious and half-welcoming
in the overlit, simple room
all hazy and warm, when I
can never go back again?

The Burren is a great
ancient grayness of rock
here in southern Ireland
where you would never expect
something so desolate

and barren to support
a single grass tuft, much less
the 300 varieties
of tiny wildflowers
people have counted, but

one morning when I got
up early to see the sunrise
skimming a part of it
I found wet pockets gathered
at dawn or in the night.

Mairena offers no bar
or café in October, only
small dogs that growl and nip
ankles as you pass by,
wondering who you are.

You're nobody, going up
to a church that isn't ringing
in this scruffy off-the-road
non-touristy village in Spain
where you happened to stop.

But it's unspoiled, the ways
and houses hardly seem
to have changed in decades,
and olive trees still rustle
until the mild wind dies.

Tonight the London Mini
is still outside #32,
the flat's window faintly
aglow with the blinds drawn,
making it fun for me

to roam this Georgian street
much like a proper bobbie
or landlord, imagining
some unreportable tryst
reaching into the night

from flat #32:
enjoyable to scope
out this elegant close
of upper Hampstead, to
guess what the others do.

The long river of Prague
flows under the Charles Bridge.
On a spring dawn I stood
with my camera alone
doing a travelogue

of emerging statuary,
outlines, a finger in the air,
a cross of thorns—they came
as brutal, vigilant figures
faithful against the sky

and waters brightening Prague.
Later my wife and I
moved among tourists and local
children to watch a woman
painting an Easter egg.

In the low-lit chapel
of bones adjoining Evora's
Igreja de Sao Francisco
that a nearly forgotten monk
of 16th century Portugal

set up for meditation
on our dusty life and death,
more than a thousand-odd
skulls pocketed and groined
into the wall (and even

a hanging skeleton)
won't take your breath away,
but they hold the mind
long after you come out
again into the sunshine.

It makes me think how long
life is, trudging from room
to room of Toltec, Aztec, Mayan
deities, figures, tombs
and trinkets a million strong!

If I were to drop dead
looking at these things
and they put me under glass
with my tote bag, would gazers
from a later period

look down at me and guess
how dazed I was? how weary?
or note how little our skill
of aesthetics has moved on
to confront or comfort us?

·

In England where we chose
to rent, bats were content
to do their dusky riffs
in summer trees of our back
garden. Now I confuse

them sitting out to gaze.
Less openly they come
as clots that man was made from,
floaters in ancient eyes,
small-fisted travelers

edgy and errandless.
Bats are the only creatures
below man that know jazz,
that know what jazz is,
can plummet and improvise.

Tate Modern. A trapezoidal
top tapering gently to
glass windows with rhomboid
facings and fluted pewter
sides just off the vertical.

It speaks of smart curating,
this almost empty box
and deadpan jut of wood
from which a purple thread
suspends its scintillating

jewel. Just a beginner,
the artist keeps it all
so chic and minimal
a passerby remarks: "This guy
drop-kicked a winner."

It may boil down to your hat,
whether it's wintry or spring-like,
jaunty or all adroop,
whether it's sitting straight
or vaguely angled. Not

perhaps for your care and quiet
response and generosity
to children and shy people
will you be remembered, as you
had hoped. Sadly your fate

may boil down to your hat,
whether it's tartan or plain
or deeply feathered, whether
you take it off as soon
as you enter—and that's that.

We've packed the Canton tray
and plates and cups and saucers
gently in cellar boxes, part
of our daughter's inheritance, thus
no longer ours in a way,

but kept some platters on
display up high to give
a kitchen overview:
blue platters back and
tilted, roughly one

per cabinet. How clear
and mild become the trees
and hills against the sky
and far flotillas riding rims
of cabinets from here.

Generally we sit out
in the warm garden, or the cool garden
nowadays, where things come to us
or others rise to get them.
Silly to worry about

the cost of all this: either
we know, or we don't care.
(Nobody ever dies here in
the ravages of war or gets
wounded.) The weather

varies from time to time.
Last summer's seemed to shower
less than usual—very fine,
almost balmy, we could hear
the crickets click and chime.

A rain begins to fall
on chairs of a summer lawn
on warm summer afternoons,
and now on summer nights
I hear its casual

patter soaking the ground,
the turn-around and road
and fields somewhere beyond
the precincts where I hold
you close. I like the sound.

We have only begun to know
our lives slipping away
like rain on summer chairs
on summer nights that began
to happen long ago.

FIVE

So here's the interior's
window, the dusty bench
and table—hardly more
than a charcoaled fireplace
sealed up for many years,

an old familiar shack.
It's been awhile since anyone
lit a night fire here.
Even spiders are gone
that got in through a crack

leaving an antimacassar
lacework loosely swaying
to our half-open door.
White webs here and there
blow like an old man's hair.

We came to another signpost
and turned to hear brook water
across something like a field—
so hard to reconstruct
the path exactly. At best

we could abandon the macadam
where once the old gentleman walked
who never spoke to us,
but that was long ago,
those summers of our Eden

when, casual or adroit,
after a long day's study
all of us swam together.
I can remember leaping
into the falls at night.

The sea being inside
the river itself, where she had caught
a little silver trout?
The day was over; I thought
of many who had died

until I was less myself
than usual—friends and men
and women of fine repute
as guides and a pretty singer
smiling across the gulf.

No, it is never enough
to remember and praise
the old cabin, whiskey and song
past midnight, two o'clock,
a girl wandering off.

Idly she doodles right
triangles, parallel bars
and sectors, blackening
tangent-circles like the eyes
of animals. At night

against her insomnia
she keeps a book of Euclid
by her bed, but never
lights the table lamp.
Instead, an architecture

blossoms in her head:
houses diminishing
down a road, a kitchen
with a gas ring, an eating
nook, and the sky red.

Did no Great Spirit come
to me and I accomplish
nothing remarkable
in a good life I wouldn't
call torrid or tiresome?

My life? My life has been
remarkably ordinary
in most respects. In most
respects, rather than out
of step I have been in.

Tonight I saw the hawks
sitting in trees—was on
my way to chaperone
a dance, a local dance,
guarding the younger folks.

Not yet the bursting flower
falling to earth. Not yet
the bursting flower falling
to earth. Not yet the bursting
flower—think of another

Easter, another year.
Think of music and wings.
Not now the bursting flower
falling to earth—at most
a light and fragrant air.

A light and fragrant air
is the most we can assume
today, and this only
at times. Don't seek the fiery
flower. It isn't here.

She found there was nothing quite
so comfortable as dawn,
a coffee cup and book,
dark islands, a flecked horizon
emerging out of the night

as the sky reddened up
to a half-pleasant draftiness
and again the old windowpanes
of squiggles and thin mullions
that would leak rain. Her cup

she'd lift to the true gods of dawn
and to lobster boats leaving.
Often it troubled her
to imagine what would come
of this place when she was gone.

Blue night with stars, yellow
awning and wall, a wanderer
leftward in the doorway
watching the waiter who takes
orders: our eyes follow

the peacefully mingled scene's
chairs and tables, wrought iron
lamp over the night-bound
customers and foreground
of rounded cobblestones.

It's 1888,
a gentle play of light
and shadow and colors by
an artist my mother loved:
a café in Arles at night.

SIX

Beacon Hill: good food
and elevator, mirrors, spiral
banister and high-spoked
circular skylight gazing
down at me since babyhood.

But what I cared for most
was not those Sunday lunches
or even the gong mannequin
my younger brother loved,
but later, as we crossed

the Charles, the evening skyline
and a first glimpse of home's
gateway to Cambridge: it
was like a little toy
lit up and truly mine.

Aunt Elsie's husband fell
from a roof he was shingling
and died. A few friends called
it fated—something about
that marriage didn't jell.

Widowed, when I was small
Aunt Elsie got me down
to New York for a musical
and subsequent jaunts, supplying
a room just off the hall.

I wondered if anyone
else ever slept there—its narrow
cot and doilied end table
and always the same book,
"You Can't Go Home Again."

You can't go home again?
But who would say so when
everything comes round
as it did, as it will again,
and you are young and clean

and to "Mood Indigo"
or maybe a late Beethoven
quartet you look up from
your paper and, out the window,
you see the initial snow

fall, as it did, again,
barely accumulating,
and any door can open
and a small son and daughter
run in, run in?

My father under the Gainsborough
and to one side of the Wyeth
reviews our inheritance
and mixes anecdotes
with his loneliness and sorrow.

We drive to visit him once
a week, my wife and I
(my brother living closer).
Like most of us he mingles
dream and reminiscence.

Even his grandfather's "The Story
of a Bad Boy," while mostly true,
trumps up some incidents,
like the oarless little schoolboy
floating out to sea.

My graying head I find
complex, though people say
I just don't look my age.
Hard to believe. Fingers
less flexible, the mind

forgetful, the poor feet
soft and sore if I press
the appropriate indents
suggesting "liver impact,"
"kidney issues." The prostate,

frankly, has given me more
runaround than everything else
combined. The later body
gets quarrelsome. It's just
that it hung so loose before.

My kohl-eyed teddy bear
is history. My mother,
tired of seeing him slouch
in the closet and surely
forgotten for many a year,

asked our cleaning lady
if she would like him, without
asking if I was finished
seeing him sit in the street light.
But I remember when he

was bigger than I was! There
he'd sit all night...And now gone.
Was that the year I decided
not to show anything, not
to feel sentimental or care?

When there is very little
time left, the clock appears
to slow down. A leaf forever
from the tree-top weaves its
slow-motion ritual

downward bough by bough
swaying through air that comes
heavier day by day now
beyond his windowsill,
and ah the hour is slow

as cones lie scattered on
soft needles, and the fir trees
gaze from their shallow roots.
Upmeadow a young boy
kicks windfalls where they've fallen.

Where the Unconscious seems
to greet us equally,
morning and evening meet.
We are the Contraries.
We are the one who dreams.

Two Japanese ladies
newly awake (it seems)
have floated down from the garden
down from the bat garden
after a shower to close

their parasols
and lift up fluted silk
kimonos now and later
undo their delicate feet
and step into pools.

Roll on, roll on, roll on
great sea, recalling sky
and wind and sun and cirrus
clouds companionable
to lovers who have known

the years and sailed away—
such crowding memories!
I conjure or imagine
a cool fog that hovers
on waves or, better, a day

of whitecaps and bright foam
and the clear distant harbor.
Roll on, roll on, great sea
for the sailor and his girl
who won't be coming home.

Only in death forgiveness
comes, and whether or not
it's real only the silent
spirits on either side,
at either end, will guess.

And yet it does feel real.
Tonight it feels as if
daylight will bring these empty
rooms to a new lightness
making the poor heart full

as one would tell a child—
not because one person is
gone and the other isn't,
but through long readiness
something is reconciled.

The first people stay alive
as they were, although gone
and no longer beautiful
and young and talking, laughing,
in tears. Yet they survive

indelible, holy, the soul
of everything I remember,
the worst and best of scattered
moments. Just the other
day it struck me the whole

puzzle works in reverse.
No wonder I feel disjointed
when I stop to contemplate
fragments of me throughout
the world—the universe.

What we have thrown away,
and what our children, too,
will throw away—those things
that enter the endless dark—
is a mystery today.

Perhaps the mystery
itself is what we threw
away—the whippoorwills
and morning glories and trees
and fireflies? Certainly

I threw away a boy
running in country dust
to the mailbox for *PM*
and its cartoon "Barnaby"
that brought a simple joy.

At night return the place-names:
Brattle Street and Rose,
Berea and Cape Elizabeth,
Tivoli, Oslo, Highgate,
Hampstead, the river Thames,

and while they often glimmer
at night or anywhere
to buffer and affirm
our little lives' appearance,
finally they don't cover

much time or area
but simply hang in air,
names as clear and fragrant
and cryptic as the Hanging
Gardens of Babylonia.

It is most true the climb
exhausted me. I fell
into a sea and floated.
I drifted outward. Plum
trees bloomed for the last time.

After a day
the misty whitecaps grew
familiar and unfamiliar.
Sky and geography loosened
and the surrounding sea

began to answer: *We*
remember, it was one
of your reveries so true
it might have been a dream.
You never felt so happy.